# Bones Beneath the Garden

Ian McNaughton

BookLeaf Publishing

India | USA | UK

Bones Beneath the Garden © 2024 Ian McNaughton

All rights reserved.

No part of this publication may be reproduced, stored in a retrieval system, or transmitted, in any form or by any means, electronic, mechanical, photocopying, recording or otherwise, without the prior written permission of the presenters.

Ian McNaughton asserts the moral right to be identified as author of this work.

Presentation by *BookLeaf Publishing*

Web: www.bookleafpub.com

E-mail: info@bookleafpub.com

ISBN: 9789360943363

First edition 2024

*I dedicate this book to Jessicamarie and
Antonio. My best friend and my lover
respectively. Two people that shaped my life at
different times and for different reasons.*

# ACKNOWLEDGEMENT

I'd like to acknowledge all the friends who've kept me going. Lucia, Joe, Matt, Trent, Ivan, Daniel, and so many more. My family as well, who although we haven't always been healthy, did not leave me out to die. We are better now, and I'm thankful for that.

# PREFACE

My life was not always easy and most of it up to this point has some drama happening. Drama isn't exactly correct, but I use it to disarm the reality. There will be many touchy subjects as they are a part of my truth. In a sense, though, I intend to celebrate these things. Pains from heartache, loss, addiction, those subjects are not off the table.

Other pieces cover the natural world as well as our relation to it. I'd like to think they are the gentler poems and help break up the poems about my life. That is to say, there is an overarching story. Details about my life in chronological order, many of them relating to the men in my life as the biggest points of conflict and impact are from them.

# Where the Monsters Are

My earliest years spent like many other
childrens' were,
  every night I kept my closet doors closed,
I thought the monsters were in there.

Myths and legends
  are all fodder for the imagination.
When you're young and naive,
  you'll believe anything.
Maybe that's why all the children closed their
closet doors
  or had their parents look under the bed.

When I was seven I asked my mother to dim the
lights.
That night would remain with me forever more.
I kept my blanket over me
  as if it were my shield.
A thin fabric that stood to be my guardian.

I recall the hours as long inhales
  and the next as extinguishing exhales.
I didn't want make a sound,
  out of fear my worst nightmare would find me.

The air was as still as a deer
  staring into oncoming headlights.
Frozen, empty, stoked with my fear.
Much like a deer, I barely moved,
  but before I knew it, I'd fall asleep.

Morning came and no monsters had gotten me,
  only the sunlight shining through the cracks of
my curtains.
That was the night I realized real monsters
  weren't hiding in my bedroom.

It would be a few more years until I learned real
monsters were the people
  that looked like you or I.
They have homes, purposes,
  and live lives contributing to society.
They could laugh, be unassuming,
  and be the first to break my heart.


I no longer feared the dark,
  monsters in my closet, or under my bed.
I feared whoever would love me next
  because one day they might not love me as they
had before.
I feared the news anchors and government
officials,

they can and do lie, cheat, and hurt us with
their ruse.

I sometimes feared my own mother,
  her anger and temper had a veracity that
silenced me.
I'd fear my father would beat me with a belt,
  or the forceful strike his palm.

So often I wished to go back to when I was
younger,
  those fears couldn't hurt or jade me.
Twenty-five years into this world and I've
realized that
  the imaginary monsters never prepared me for
the real pain.
But that's okay.
I'm learning and growing.
I'm still afraid but I have courage and
confidence.

Deep breathes, the sun is rising again,
  I've got a new day.
I've made it through another night.

# Mother's

He wore mother's heels, her nice jewelry, too.
Stole her earrings and tried on the cheap
mascara.
He wore the wedding dress for playtime at
school.

They told him to try the pinstripe suit, but alas it
was ugly, they lacked appeal.
The finer things in his life were feminine.
Soft and flowing fabric, the synthetic doll hair
that swayed in the water at bath time,
and girls toys from fast food kid's meals.

He liked his mother's company to his father's.
This was before he learned to be more afraid of
her than him.
For so much of his childhood he was his
mother's baby boy.
As his father would come to say,

"The daughter we never had."

# Paradise Lost

Stung by words I had not known,
"Gay," "Faggot," "Cock sucker,"
I was a child, only eight passes around the sun.
Yet systemic hate made its way in my life.
I grew to fear the playground as it became a
battlefield.
A no man's land for my mental well being.
My bedroom, a sanctuary, though my thoughts
sought to hurt me.
I was unable to process the hate I received
for actions I was coerced into.
Heinous acts a child shouldn't know about at
eight,
but alas, innocence was lost.
My first exposure to a cruel and unjust world,
I was labeled gay and that was a problem?
I couldn't have known, though.
Rumors spread like wildfire,
no one believed me when I tried to defend
myself.
"Someone else forced himself onto me,"
"My brother and I never had sex,"
"I'm not gay, I swear I'm straight."
He abused my innocence for his pleasure
and weaponized my weakness to save his skin.

A fourteen year old neighboring boy got away with
raping an eight year old.
Damaging my ability to trust, hurting me in long
lasting ways.
I didn't feel safe, but I had to fit in.
There would be no comeuppance for him,
there would be a long road to love for me.

# Survival

A forest otherwise quiet and alone,
  two souls from different walks of life meet.
Eye to eye the huntress stared
  locking gaze with innocence.
An animal, a fraction of her age,
  she aimed and readied.
The beast staring,
  unaware of the tool the human holds.
Her arrow striking the beast,
  red glittering the foliage.
It fell and cried out.
She would have food, fur, and weapons of bone.
Ancient and carnal,
  cyclical and unforgiving.
The remains of the beast bring forth life and
fertile land.
Another life cut short,
  but nary a soul is useless.
Flowering from the once spry beast.
Even in death life finds a way.

# Acceptance

I would come to realize that I was different.
Not because the others bullied me,
but because I did like boys.
I was around eleven when these thoughts came
about.
They were right in a way,
I wasn't straight,
They were just right in hindsight.
That doesn't absolve them of their crimes.
This child was still damaged,
thrust into a depression and darkness for their
acts.
Innocence was still lost,
playtime was still muddled with self doubt and
fear.
I was damaged, but coming to terms with the
truth.
The very truth that hurt, confused, and isolated
me.
There was so much to process,
so much to consider and reflect on.
Months would pass,
each night staying up late with my own
thoughts.
Who would I one day love?

How would I love in the state I'm in?
I cried so many nights, all alone in my bedroom.
I wished there had been monsters in my closet,
Maybe then I would have had company.

# Bones Beneath the Garden

Gnawed bones and flesh mangled,
beasts feast and left engorged.
Remains integrating into the soil,
a land laid in beauty and life.

Yet humanity's hubris strong and willing
brought rise to structures.
Towers and spires caressing the skies.
Illuminated at nightfall, the stars disappear.
And ancient giants rooted are denied further
growth and reduced to dust.

Denying nature it's due diligence
Below it all bones prevail; microfauna flourish,
and waters still thrive.

Hubris one day met with humility.
For now the bones wait.
Beneath gardens and suburban plots,
occupied by a people unaware of their treasure.
Propagandized and coerced, due to pay for sins
all the same.

# Silent Night

Moonlight embraces the insects
glowing against the forest's backdrop.

A calm, overwhelming sensation,
the privilege to feel safe.

A mother lays and gives birth.

New life cries and opens its eyes for the first
time.

The fawn stares into the sky,
stars reflecting their stories into its innocence.

For one night it would be quiet.

Machines of war lay asleep on the burrows,
land blackened from their foil.

Unjustly it would seem to be born now.

Alive in time to witness atrocity.

This child without a reminder of better times.

The mother left exhausted, she dies.

Blacken are her lungs,
weakened from a lack of food,
injured from stray fire.

Barely able to walk, the fawn begins.

Life exists and hope wallows behind.

At last, this wasted land brings life.

What a shame it is, though,
to be born at the wrong time.

# I Said It

My father laughed at the thought,
"You can't be gay."
All my consideration, sleepless nights,
the time spent accepting myself first,
suddenly it meant nothing.
My anxiety insurmountable,
my hopes and expectations shot down
Like a skeet on its first flight.
My heart blurred
my legs told me to run,
so I did.
The same red haired friend there to support me
chased me and brought me back.
My father insisting I'm too young to know what
gay is,
I sat there in a darkness only I could see.
My stomach afloat, my tears the water it sailed
on,
my body the anchor,
heavy.
I'm not too young, I can't be.
With my childhood ripped away from me,
too young was not a liberty I was granted.

# Flockless

Rose colored lips and cheeks blush against pale
skin.
Small, vulnerable, left to learn from the world
around her.
A lamb in lamb's clothing, she was nothing
more than impressionable.
Born to loving but unequipped parents.
Unremarkable, unassuming, ripe for the taking.
A girl lost on herself while others stole her skin.
Removing the parts of her until she was

                                 no  longer

w h o l e.

Shearling gone that otherwise kept her warm.
She would lay hollowed and alone on the bed.

Her parents trying until their frustrations boiled
over,
Lashing out on the lamb who could

                                 no  longer

p r o t e c t  herself.

Isolated and removed from once loving
memories.
This lamb would

                                            no  longer
remain  i n n o c e n t.

Forcing the hands of men to supply her with
love and sustenance.
Finding the reasons she needed to continue
breathing.
Halfway homes and stray dogs, the city
unforgiving.
Her parents never looked, the wolves passed her
by, and men preyed.
As she lay to rest and buried under a headstone
with no name,
a stranger could only wonder why this once frail
lamb was

                                            no  longer
l o v e d.

# The Boy on the Farm

He lived only a couple hours away,
  on a farm with his family.
We never met, though.
Neither of us had a car,
  and we didn't tell our parents.

We met online,
  on tumblr, via dubious means.
That would be the first time I love someone.
It was an innocent love,
  the innocence I didn't get to have for years.

We were only thirteen but for once it felt good
  to be me,
    to be gay.
We'd facetime and relax together on camera.

He had this curly hair,
  light brown skin that looked so soft.
I regret not being able to meet him and feel for
myself.

He'd play his guitar and I'd listen.
We'd talk about our days,

he was rambunctious and was always up to
something nefarious.

I knew it wouldn't last,
  the first ones rarely do,
    but knowing that there was at least one
partner for me
      made me feel more whole.
More certain that who I am was correct.

I loved him, and I hoped he loved me, too.

# 24%

Sterile space and white lights,
  bodies moving in urgence.
Time slows down yet moves too quickly,
  alarms sound in emergence.

Twenty-four percent is all they have,
  a number smaller each second.
Life slipping away

        away

          away,

  awaiting some god's reckon.

Post haste they move,
  and get to work on his chest.
Unhealthy and old
  in cardiac arrest.

Twenty-four percent chance
  to get him back.
Seconds to minutes,
  taking turns and causing cracks.

Ribs splitting in
  one,
        two,
          or three.
This visceral sensation,
  bruising pools like filigree.

The chances are slim,
  never in our favor.
Yet steadfast they work,
  resolve to non waiver.

No matter the creed nor cast,
  this man has to live.
Against time and odds,
  these workers are resistive.

Twenty-four percent chance,
  the best chance they had.
With worked tired and in tears,
  this man lay there shirt unclad.

A man would yell
  for his love to appear.
Running into the room,
  it would be made clear.

With tears swelling from all around,

they again deny poor health's outrance.
His love would live,
   off a twenty-four percent chance.

# How We Were

I envy us and the way we used to be.
Comfortable in our depression,
  sad together and trauma split evenly.
The most dramatic part of our lives
  was who and why we loved boys who weren't
good to us.
I remember that rufescent night,
  red hair, shirts, pants, thighs.
Up late at night sharing secrets,
  spilling blood in mutual turmoil.
It was easy, no pressure to be great,
  no need to live our lives unlike we were then.
To Ivan, the friend who witnessed my first
darknesses.
Just us and the razors we kept
  hidden from the rest of the world.
We kept ourselves hidden too,
  but to each other we mattered.
Nothing to hide, everything in the open,
  and every part of ourselves is loved by the
other.

# Four Years

Alarms blaring and a mother's call,
another morning that wasn't hoped for.
Morning dew, quiet and cold,
the bus stop is no different.
Concrete steps and large glass doors,
sizing up expectations.
For four years I had to be ready.

Lockers slamming, bells ring, sneakers marking
the gymnasium floor.
Violins and children sing, pencils break, and
students jest over lunch.
For four years I was tired.

Everyday waking up wishing I hadn't,
feigning happiness to avoid confrontation.
On the stage I was alive, but those long
rehearsals ate me alive.
In costume and voice I was someone new,
but behind it all I reminded isolated.
For four years I never felt right.

Few highs and mostly lows,
Edges and fine lines painted,
permanent.

Occasionally genuine laughter,
affections from peers and friends.
Sparks and small flames illuminating the
darkness.
For four years I tried to find hope.

Within time the lights would shine on me.
Warmth and comfort,
reliability and consolation.
I was cared for, treated with patience.
Finally I could wake up to love after
falling asleep to despair.
For two years I could find time to grow

# The Last Time I Saw You

I thought you were
  a perfect representation of my love.

I was wrong.
Trust broken, love used, and my body   abused.
Every part of me knowing it was wrong,
  but my need for your attachment was greater
than my self preservation.

Made to sleep on the cold hardwood floor,
  a likeness to your love for me.
Only sharing your bed for sex.
Three times this would happen.

Sent out in the middle of the night,
  into the cold, snow draped city.
You had last minute plans the next morning,
  those plans more important than the safety of a
teenager you let pleasure you.

Alone and isolated again.
Reminded that naivety and infatuation
  result in dissatisfaction.

Looking over a bridge,

the cold hard floor could be the last thing I feel.
A final reminder of who I loved, but tried too
hard to know how.

Your words echoed in my head,
"I want to love you but I don't know how."
And should that be the last thing I let ring in my
mind,
  at least if you've come from you.

# Purpose

Cries and screams break the silence
  otherwise kept by thick snow.
A new mother lay tired,
  in embrace with life she bore.
Skin to skin, warmed by the parka,
  the cold air visualizing their breath.

Blood spilled, dying the perfect white a
  vibrant red.
This birth is a reminder of nature's intent,
  its design.
Painful, unruly, beautiful, and in this instance,
  maternal.

Her purposed realized,
  to guardian this child and keep her safe.
The world has yet to show forgiveness,
  but briefly time would slow down.
At last, it would be time to rest,
  to finally set aside the spears and sleep.

# A Bottle of Anemoia

You fooled me with your camouflage,
  a predator disguised as a lover.
With teeth dull and wit unaware,
  your needs seemed simple.

Yet there I was, alone in your bed,
  waiting on you to drive home after the highs.
Revelry always came before me.
The highs before the second choice cut at home.
Prey when the drinks and late night fast food
weren't enough.
Chaser for your cheap vodka.

Finally I was no longer food,
  I demanded to eat in return.
Without regard you left me to starve.
But I wouldn't starve.
  I would drink too.

Getting so drunk I'd lose feeling in my
appendages,
  the numb replaced the frustrations of you,
    keeping away good memories to keep myself
safe.

I can't feel my groin, so I forget what sex with
you is like,
   nor my fingertips so I forget what your skin felt
like,
   nor my lips, so I forget what your lips felt
like.

I relied on your sensibilities when you had none,
   on your presence knowing revelry was always
before me,
   on your sympathy when you got so inebriated
you lost it.

So used to being a second choice that I became
my own.
It reminded me what I meant to you.
Flush and numb from the alcohol,
   I wonder why you chose its warmth over me.

# Mosaicists

I am a mosaic of all the people who have met
me.
A piece of art painted by those who have sought
to need and want me.
People who gave me their time, and showed me
humanity.
An amalgamation of hundreds of peoples' effort
to impact and change me
From those who meant me no love,
  and those who meant me no harm,
    hurting me in ways that made me better.
Each stroke of a brush or knife further creates a
me that is ready.
When the mosaic stops, I do not know but when
it does,
  I know to be at peace with the art I became.

# We Stopped

11:30pm, I opened the door to your message.
A quick hookup and it would be time for bed.
When I saw you, I was taken aback.
My age, a bit shorter, charismatic smile;
  where I expected to see what I had seen so
many times before,
  I saw you.
Handsome, a barely trimmed mustache and
stubble.
You entered my home with the same intention.

When we arrived to my bedroom the usual
response wasn't spoken,
  "How do you want to do this?"
 Instead, an immediate interest in my animals,
  who, as I raised them,
  are an extension of me.

You took interest in me past my body.
Our lips met after the conversation,
  and it felt right so soon.

Our bodies together, soft and warm.
Before we continued we stopped and talked
about my books.

Talk of literature and a shared hobby took over.
Your interest and inquisitiveness into my life
made me excited to speak.

Your knowledge caught me off guard,
  I was relieved to be challenged.
Our bodies soon compressed again as we
embraced.
Although we had just met,
  your body felt right with mine.

As you were on top of me, we stopped,
  philosophy came to mind.
Where I was physically aroused,
  I am now mentally so.
Our favorite philosophers, ethics, thoughts,
politics.

Our bodies soon again together,
  swapping positions with a negative space
between us.
A feeling so natural we couldn't deny our need
for embrace.
We recklessly obliged and finished.

I collapsed backward, laying there exhausted.
I asked about your pronouns and we talked
about gender.

That night was supposed to be a quick hook-up.
Alas, it would turn out to be the night I met the
love of my life.

# Respite

Shroud covers the sky
Trees sparkle with stars high above.
Serenity, closure.
Another day met with uncertainty.
Often the hardships of this earth
  make us forget how to stop.
This child will soon know, as her mother does
now,
  but for now, she sleeps.
Bare bones scattered; the venison devoured.
The fire cracking and her mother sits awake,
  whittling the same bones to create weapons.
Protecting her kin as she promised to
  until she embraces the earth like prey before
her.
What hardships they have faced are behind
them.
For now, they can rest,
  knowing that another unpromised day has
passed.

# Kairosclerosis

Silence enveloped the house.
The only sounds to be made come from them or
I.
Enjoying food while flying with the gods.
Home starting feeling like this place,
     quaint and slow,
      two souls
united.
Both a quarter century old,
     but the feelings have
been felt for thousands of years.
Safety, loved, comforted, as if reality has set on
     and I'm not on the losing
side this time.
Nor fear is felt, nor uncertainty, nor distrust.
The monsters in my head have been silent.
I'm where I'm meant to be,
     who I am meant to be
with.

I'm happy.

www.ingramcontent.com/pod-product-compliance
Lightning Source LLC
Chambersburg PA
CBHW061729130726
47996CB00006B/2570